# Miss Bea's Colours

M000086214

## Louisa Harding

ROWAN

Hello, who's that running down the lane?
It's Owen with a gold balloon

Gold Star sweater instructions page 28

Miss Bea is busy cleaning cobwebs with her pink feather duster

'The leaves keep falling' Owen says
sweeping up with his orange handled broom

With her yellow gloves and bucket
Miss Bea uses lots of soapy water

'The plants have fallen over'
Joe stands them up in his green Wheelbarrow

Alice uses a silver watering can 'splash' the water has made a big puddle

Silver splash Sweater instructions page 38

'Look at me splashing' Miss Bea squeals
red wellies keep her feet dry

Hearts Sweater instructions page 40

Joe is digging in the soil
he is planting flowers in a big brown pot

Alice cries 'wheee'
her purple windmill spins as she runs

Miss Bea puts up her blue Umbrella,
'it's started to rain, bye bye'

Umbrella Sweater instructions page 46

# The Knitting Patterns
## Information Page

## Introduction
The knitwear in 'Miss Bea's Colours' has been designed with beginner knitters in mind. The garment shapes are simple to knit and all can be knitted in one colour.

Inspired to pick up your knitting needles we hope you find the instructions easy to understand and the guide to Knitting Techniques a helpful resource to follow.

## The knitting patterns
Each pattern has a chart and simple written instructions that have been colour coded making the different sizes easier to identify. E.g. if you are knitting age 2–3 years follow the instructions in red where you are given a choice.

The patterns are laid out as follows:

## Age/Size Diagrams
The ages given and the corresponding diagrams are a guide only. The measurements for each knitted piece are shown in a size diagram at the start of every pattern. As all children vary make sure you choose the right garment size, do this by measuring an item of your child's clothing you like the fit of. Choose the instruction size accordingly. If still unsure, knit a larger size, as children always grow.

## Yarn
This indicates the amount of yarn needed to complete the design.
If the garment is striped or colour blocked you will have an amount for each colour used.

## Needles
Listed are the suggested knitting needles used to make the garment. The smaller needles are usually used for edgings or ribs, the larger needles for the main body fabric.

## Buttons/Zips
This indicates the number of buttons or length of zip needed to fasten the finished garment.

## Tension
Tension is the single most important factor when you begin knitting. The fabric tension is written for example as 20 sts x 28 rows to 10cm measured over stocking stitch using 4 mm (US 6) needles. Each pattern is worked out mathematically, if the correct tension is not achieved the garment pieces will not measure the size stated in the diagram.

Before embarking on knitting your garment we recommend you check your tension as follows: Using the needle size given cast on 5 –10 more stitches than stated in the tension, and work 5 –10 more rows. When you have knitted your tension square lay it on a flat surface, place a rule or tape measure horizontally, count the number of stitches equal to the distance of 10cm. Place the measure vertically and count the number of rows, these should equal the tension given in the pattern. If you have too many stitches to 10cm, try again using a thicker needle, if you have too few stitches to 10cm use a finer needle.

**Note:** Check your tension regularly as you knit, once you become relaxed and confident with your knitting, your tension can change.

## Back
This is the start of your pattern. Following the colour code for your chosen size, you will be instructed how many stitches to cast on and to work from chart and written instructions as follows:

## Knitting from charts
Each square on a chart represents one stitch; each line of squares indicates a row of knitting. When working from the chart, read odd numbered rows (right side of fabric) from right to left and even numbered rows (wrong side of fabric) from left to right.

Each separate colour used is given a letter and on some charts a corresponding symbol. The different stitches used are also represented by a symbol, e.g. knit and purl, a key to the symbols is with each chart.

## Front (fronts) and sleeves
The pattern continues with instructions to make these garment pieces.

## Pressing
Once you have finished knitting and before you begin to complete the garment it is important that all pieces are pressed, see page 48 for more details.

## Neckband (front bands)
This instruction tells you how to work any finishing off needed to complete your garment, such as knitting a neckband on a sweater or edgings on a cardigan. Once you have completed all the knitting you can beg to make up your garment, see page 48 for making up instructions.

## Abbreviations
In the pattern you will find some of the most common words used have been abbreviated, these are listed below:

| | |
|---|---|
| **K** | knit |
| **P** | purl |
| **st(s)** | stitches |
| **inc** | increase(e)(ing) |
| **dec** | decrease(e)(ing) |
| **st st** | stocking stitch (right side row knit, wrong side row purl) |
| **garter st** | garter stitch (knit every row) |
| **beg** | begin(ning) |
| **foll** | follow(ing) |
| **rem** | remain(ing) |
| **rev** | reverse(ing) |
| **rep** | repeat |
| **alt** | alternate |
| **cont** | continue |
| **patt** | pattern |
| **tog** | together |
| **cm** | centimetres |
| **in(s)** | inch(es) |
| **RS** | right side |
| **WS** | wrong side |
| **K2tog** | knit two sts together to make one stitch |
| **tbl** | through back of loop |
| **yo** | yarn over, bring yarn over needle before working next st to create an extra loop. |

# Knitting Techniques
## A simple learn to knit guide

## Introduction

Using illustrations and simple written instructions we have put together a beginners guide to knitting. With a basic knowledge of the simplest stitches you can create your own unique handknitted garments.

When you begin to knit you feel very clumsy, all fingers and thumbs. This stage passes as confidence and experience grows. Many people are put off hand knitting thinking that they are not using the correct techniques of holding needles, yarn or working of stitches, all knitters develop their own style, so please persevere.

## Casting On – This is the term used for making a row of stitches; the foundation row for each piece of knitting.

Make a slip knot. Slip this onto a needle. This is the basis of the two casting on techniques as shown below.

## Thumb Cast On – This method uses only one needle and gives a neat, but elastic edge. Make a slip knot 1 metre from the cut end of the yarn, you use this length to cast on the stitches. For a knitted piece, the length between cut end and slip knot can be difficult to judge, allow approx 3 times the width measurement.

| | | | | | |
|---|---|---|---|---|---|
| Make a slip knot approx 1 metre from the end of the yarn, with ball yarn to your right. | 2. Hold needle in RH. With the cut end of yarn held in LH, wrap yarn around your thumb from left to right anti-clockwise to front. | 3. Insert RH needle into yarn around thumb, take yarn attached to ball around the back of RH needle to front. | 4. Draw through needle to make a loop. | 5. Pull on both ends of yarn gently. Creating a stitch on right hand needle. | 6. Repeat from 2. until the required number of stitches has been cast on. |

## Cable Cast On – This method uses two needles; it gives a firm neat finish. It is important that you achieve an even cast on, this may require practice.

| | | | | | |
|---|---|---|---|---|---|
| With slip knot on LH needle, insert RH needle. Take yarn behind RH needle; bring yarn forward between needles. | 2. Draw the RH needle back through the slip knot, making a loop on RH needle with yarn. | 3. Slip this loop onto left hand needle; taking care not to pull the loop too tight. | 4. Insert the RH needle between the two loops on LH needle. Take yarn behind RH needle; bring forward, between needles. | 5. Draw through the RH needle making a loop as before. Slip this stitch onto LH needle. | 6. Repeat from 4. until the required number of stitches has been cast on. |

# How to Knit -
The knit stitch is the simplest to learn. By knitting every row you create garter stitch and the simplest of all knitted fabrics. Garter stitch is reversible and does not curl, it is often used for edgings and bands.

 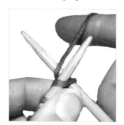   

1. Hold the needle with the cast-on stitches in LH. Insert RH needle into first stitch.

2. Take yarn around the back of RH needle, bring yarn forward between needles.

3. Draw the RH needle through the stitch. Drop loop on LH needle

4. Making a loop on RH needle with yarn. One stitch made.

5. Repeat to the end of the row.

# How to Purl -
The purl stitch is a little more complicated to master. Using a combination of knit and purl stitches together forms the bases of most knitted fabrics. The most common fabric knitted is stocking stitch, this is created when you knit 1 row, then purl 1 row.

1. Hold the needle with stitches on in LH and with yarn at the front of work, insert RH needle into front of stitch.

2. Take yarn around the back of RH needle, bring yarn to front.

3. Draw the needle through from front to back, making a loop on RH needle.

4. Slip the stitch onto right hand needle. Drop loop on LH needle.

5. Repeat to the end of the row.

# Knit 2, Purl 2 Rib -
This uses a combination of knit and purl stitches worked on the same row of knitting to create an elastic fabric.
Cast on an even number of stitches (a multiple of 4). With cast on stitches in left hand work as follows: **Row 1**: knit 2 stitches, purl 2 stitches, repeat this action to the end of the row, ending with purl 2 stitches. **Row 2**: Knit 2 stitches, Purl 2 stitches. To create the rib, always knit stitches that were purled on the previous row and vice versa. You can vary ribs by working different combinations of stitches, e.g. knit 1, purl 1 rib, this creates a tight rib or knit 4, purl 4 rib which creates a looser fabric.

# Joining in a new yarn -
A new ball of yarn can be joined in on either a right side or a wrong side row, but to give a neat finish it is important yo do this at the start of a row. Simply drop the old yarn, start knitting with the new ball, then after a few stitches tie the two ends together in a temporary knot. These ends are then sewn into the knitting at the making up stage, see page 48. Stripes are the simplest way of creating interest and variety to a garment. Join in the new colour as you would join in a new yarn and make the stripes as narrow or wide as you like.

# ecreasing One Stitch (K2tog) – This is the method used to reduce the number of stitches in a row. Worked at the edge to shape a neck with a yo (yarn over) to create buttonholes. This method can be worked on both knit and purl side of fabric.

Hold the needle with
e stitches on in LH,
sert RH needle into first
o stitches.

2. Take yarn around back of RH needle, bring yarn forward between needles.

3. Draw the RH needle through both stitches.

4. Making a loop on RH needle. One stitch made by knitting two stitches together.

# ncreasing One Stitch – This method of increasing stitches is used to shape side edges, it can be worked at the end of either a knit or purl row.

 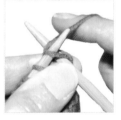    

Hold the needle with
e stitches on in LH,
sert RH needle into first
tch.

2. Take yarn around back of RH needle, bring yarn forward between needles.

3. Draw through RH needle making loop, one stitch made. Do not drop stitch off LH needle.

4. Reinsert RH needle into the back of same stitch.

5. Take yarn around back of RH needle, bring yarn forward between needles.

6. Draw through RH needle making loop. Two stitches made by knitting into front and back of one stitch.

# asting Off – This is the method of securing stitches at the top of your knitted fabric. It is important that the cast off edge should by elastic like the rest of the bric; if you find that your cast off is too tight, try using a larger needle. You can cast off knitwise (as illustrated), purlwise, or in a combination of stitches, such as rib.

Hold the needle with
e stitches on in LH, knit
e first stitch.

2. Knit the next stitch from LH needle, two stitches on RH needle.

3. Using the point of LH needle; insert into first stitch on RH needle.

4. Take the first stitch over the second stitch.

5. One stitch on right hand needle.

6. Rep from 2. until one stitch on RH needle. Cut yarn, draw cut end through last stitch to secure.

# Gold Star Sweater

Age    1-2 year    2-3 years    3-4 years

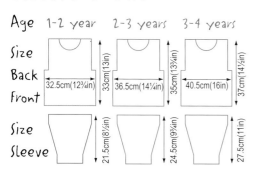

| Size | | |
|---|---|---|
| Back | | |
| Front | 32.5cm(12¾in) 33cm(13in) | 36.5cm(14¼in) 35cm(13¾in) | 40.5cm(16in) 37cm(14½in) |

| Size | | |
|---|---|---|
| Sleeve | 21.5cm(8½in) | 24.5cm(9¾in) | 27.5cm(11in) |

## Yarn
Rowan Handknit Cotton x 50g balls
Ice Water    6        6        7

## Needles
1 pair 3 ¼ mm (US 3) needles for edging
1 pair 4mm (US 6) needles for main body

## Tension
20 sts and 28 rows to 10cm measured over stocking stitch using 4 mm (US 6) needles

## Note Textured star is worked on front of sweater only

## Back
Using 3 ¼ mm (US 3) needles, cast on 65,73,81 sts and work from chart and written instructions as folls:
**Chart row 1:** Knit.
**Chart row 2:** Knit.
Cont in garter st until chart row 6 completed.
Change to 4mm (US 6) needles and cont to work in st st only as folls:
**Chart row 7:** Knit.
**Chart row 8:** Purl.
Work until chart row 58,60,64 completed.

## Shape armhole
Cast off 6 sts at the beg next 2 rows.
(53,61,69 sts)
Work until chart row 94,100,106 completed.
## Shape shoulders and back neck
Cast off 4,5,6, sts at the beg next 2 rows.
**Chart row 97,103,109:** Cast off 4,5,6 sts, knit until 6,7,8 sts on RH needle, turn and leave rem sts on a holder.
**Chart row 98,104,110:** Cast off 3 sts, purl to end.
Cast off rem 3,4,5 sts.
Slip centre 25,27,29 sts onto a holder, rejoin yarn to rem sts and knit to end.
(10,12,14 sts)
**Chart row 98,104,110:** Cast off 4,5,6 sts, purl to end. (6,7,8 sts)
**Chart row 99,105,111:** Cast off 3 sts, knit to end.
Cast off rem 3,4,5 sts.

## Front
Work as for back until chart row 30 completed.
Chart row 31: K32,36,40, P1, K32,36,40.
Chart row 32: Purl.
Chart row 33: K31,35,39, P1, K1, P1, K31,35,39.
Chart row 34: Purl.
Cont to work textured star from chart as indicated until chart row 58,60,64 completed.
## Shape armhole
Keeping textured star patt correct, cast off 6 sts at the beg next 2 rows. (53,61,69 sts)
Cont in patt without further shaping until chart row 90,96,102 completed.
## Shape front neck
**Chart row 91,97,103:** Knit 17,20,23 sts, turn and leave rem sts on a holder.
**Chart row 92,98,104:** Cast off 4 sts, purl to end.
Dec 1 st at neck edge on next 2 rows.
(11,14,17 sts)
## Shape Shoulder
**Chart row 95,101,107:** Cast off 4,5,6 sts at beg next row and foll alt row.
Purl 1 row.
Cast off rem 3,4,5 sts.
Slip centre 19,21,23 sts onto a holder, rejoin yarn to rem sts and knit to end. (17,20,23 sts)
Purl 1 row
**Chart row 93,99,105:** Cast off 4 sts, knit to end.
Dec 1 st at neck edge on next 2 rows. (11,14,17 sts)
## Shape shoulder
**Chart row 96,102,108:** Cast off 4,5,6 sts at beg next row and foll alt row.
Knit 1 row. Cast off rem 3,4,5 sts.

## Sleeves (both alike)
Using 3 ¼ mm (US 3) needles cast on 33,35,37 sts and work from chart and written instructions as folls:
**Chart row 1:** Knit.
**Chart row 2:** Knit.
Cont in garter st until chart row 6 completed.
Change to 4 mm (US 6) needles and cont to work in st st only as folls:
**Chart row 7:** Inc into first st, knit to last st, inc into last st. (35,37,39 sts)
**Chart row 8:** Purl.
Cont in st st from chart, shaping sides by inc as indicated to 51,55,59 sts.
Work without further shaping until chart row 62,70,78 completed.
Cast off .

## Press all pieces as shown in making up instructions, page 48.

## Neckband
Join right shoulder seam using backstitch.
Using 3 ¼ mm (US 3) needles pick up and knit 10 sts down left front neck, knit across 19,21,23 sts on holder, pick up and knit 10 sts to shoulder and 3 sts down right back neck, knit across 25,27,29 sts on holder, pick up and knit 3 sts to shoulder. (70,74,78 sts)
Knit 4 rows.
Cast off knitwise on WS.
Complete sweater as shown in making up instructions page 48.

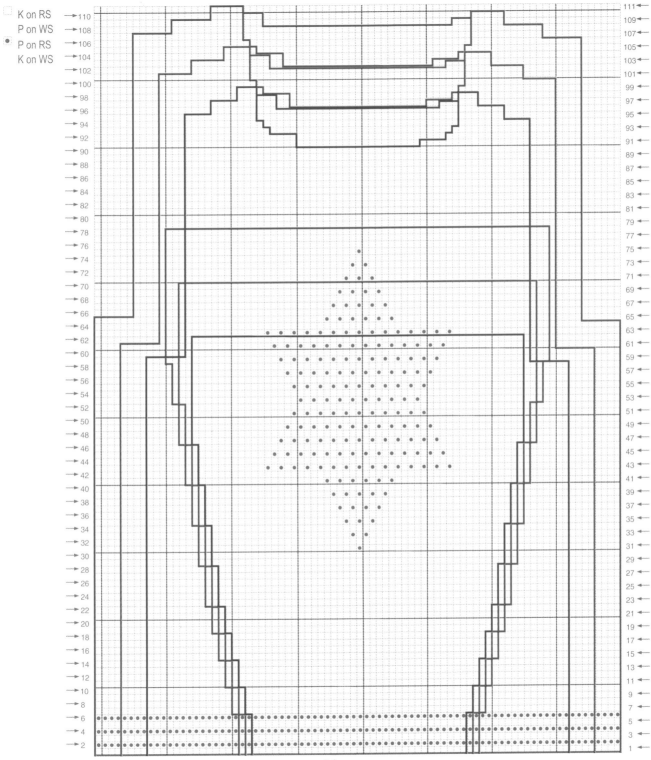

29

# Fleur Cardigan

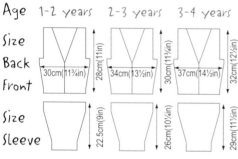

| Age | 1-2 years | 2-3 years | 3-4 years |
|---|---|---|---|
| Size Back Front | 30cm(11¾in) 28cm(11in) | 34cm(13½in) 30cm(11¾in) | 37cm(14½in) 32cm(12½in) |
| Size Sleeve | 22.5cm(9in) | 26cm(10½in) | 29cm(11½in) |

## Yarn
Rowan Wool Cotton x 50g balls

| Ice | 4 | 4 | 5 |
|---|---|---|---|

## Needles
1 pair 3 ¼ mm (US 3) needles for edging
1 pair 4mm (US 6) needles for main body

## Buttons   4

## Tension
22 sts and 30 rows to 10cm measured over textured pattern using 4 mm (US 6) needles

## Back
Using 3 ¼ mm (US 3) needles cast on 56,64,72 sts and work from chart and written instructions as folls:
**Chart row 1:** Knit.
**Chart row 2:** Knit.
Work these 2 rows once more
Change to 4mm (US 6) needles and work in textured flower pattern as indicated on chart.
Work until chart row 8 completed.
**Chart row 9:** Inc into first st, patt to last st, inc into last st. (58,66,74 sts)

Cont from chart shaping sides by inc as indicated to 66,74,82 sts.
Work without further shaping until chart row 44,48,52 completed.
### Shape armhole
Cast off 6 sts at the beg next 2 rows. (54,62,70 sts)
Work until chart row 84,90,96 completed.
### Shape shoulders and back neck
Cast off 4,5,6, sts at the beg next 2 rows.
**Chart row 89,93,99:** Cast off 4,5,6 sts, patt until 7,8,9 sts on RH needle, turn and leave rem sts on a holder.
**Chart row 90,94,100:** Cast off 3 sts, patt to end.
Cast off rem 4,5,6 sts.
Rejoin yarn and cast off centre 24,26,28 sts, patt to end. (11,13,15 sts)
**Chart row 88,94,100:** Cast off 4,5,6 sts, patt to end. (7,8,9 sts)
**Chart row 89,95,101:** Cast off 3 sts, patt to end.
Cast off rem 4,5,6 sts.

## Left Front
Using 3 ¼ mm (US 3) needles cast on 28,32,36 sts and work from chart and written instructions as folls:
**Chart row 1:** Knit.
**Chart row 2:** Knit.
Work these 2 rows once more
Change to 4mm (US 6) needles and work in textured flower pattern as indicated on chart.
Work until chart row 8 completed.
**Chart row 9:** Inc into first st, patt to end. (29,33,37 sts)
Cont from chart, shaping side edge by inc as indicated to 33,37,41 sts.
Work without further shaping until chart row 44,48,52 completed.
### Shape armhole and front neck
Cast off 6 sts at the beg next row, patt to last 2 sts, K2tog. (26,30,34 sts)
Cont to dec at neck edge as indicated to 12,15,18 sts.
Work without further shaping until chart row 84,90,96 completed.
### Shape shoulder
Cast off 4,5,6, sts at the beg next row and foll alt row.
Work 1 row
Cast off rem 4,5,6 sts.

## Right Front
Using 3 ¼ mm (US 3) needles cast on 28,32,36 sts and work from chart and written instructions as folls:
**Chart row 1:** Knit.
**Chart row 2:** Knit.
Work these 2 rows once more

Change to 4mm (US 6) needles and work in textured flower pattern and complete to match left front, foll cha for right front and reversing shaping.

## Sleeves (both alike)
Using 3 ¼ mm (US 3) needles and cast on 38,40,42 s and work from chart and written instructions as folls:
**Chart row 1:** Knit.
**Chart row 2:** Knit.
Work these 2 rows once more.
Change to 4 mm (US 6) needles and cont to work in s st as folls:
**Chart row 5:** Knit.
**Chart row 6:** Purl.
**Chart row 7:** Inc into first st, patt to last st, inc into las st. (40,42,44 sts)
**Chart row 8:** Patt to end.
Cont from chart, shaping sides by inc as indicated to 58,62,66 sts.
Work without further shaping until chart row 68,78,88 completed.
Cast off.

## Press
all pieces as shown in making up instructions, page 48.

## Frontband
Join both shoulder seams using backstitch.
With RS of right front facing and using 3 ¼ mm (US 3) needles pick up and knit 33,35,37 sts from cast on edg to start of neck shaping, 37,39,41 sts up right front nec slope to shoulder, 28,30,32 sts across back neck, pick up and knit 37,39,41 sts down left front neck slope, and 33,35,37 sts to end. (168,178,188 sts)
**Buttonhole row (WS):** Knit 135,145,152 sts, (yo, K2tog, K8,8,9) 3 times, yo, K2tog, K1.
**Next row:** Knit.
Cast off knitwise.
Sew on buttons to correspond with buttonholes.
Complete cardigan as shown in making up instructions page 48.

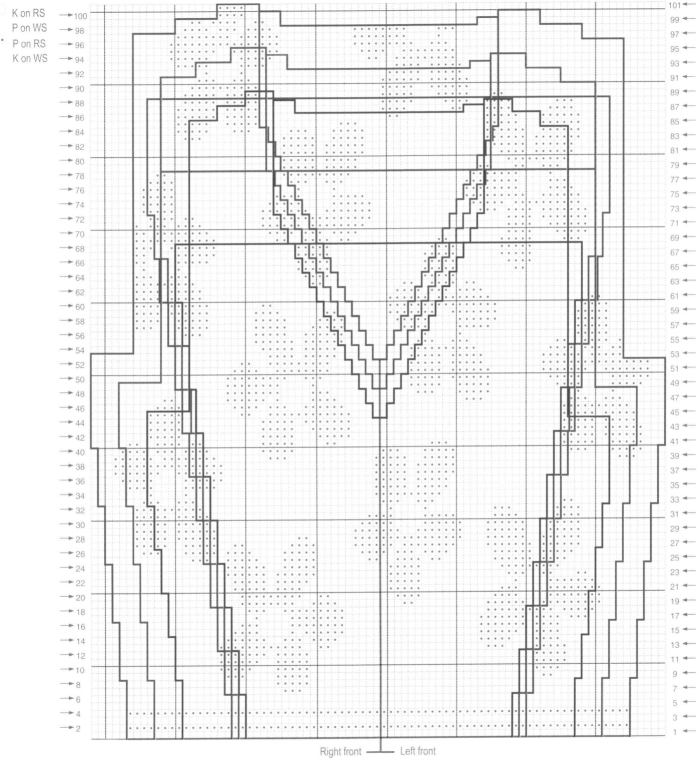

K on RS
P on WS
P on RS
K on WS

Right front — Left front

31

# Sweeping Star Jacket

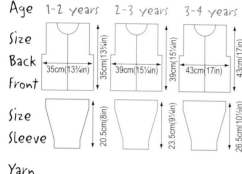

| Age | 1-2 years | 2-3 years | 3-4 years |
|-----|-----------|-----------|-----------|

Size
Back
Front

35cm(13¾in)  35cm(13¾in)
39cm(15¼in)  39cm(15¼in)
43cm(17in)  43cm(17in)

Size
Sleeve

20.5cm(8in)  23.5cm(9¼in)  26.5cm(10½in)

## Yarn
Rowan Handknit Cotton x 50g balls
Blue          7          7          8

## Needles
1 pair 3 ¼ mm (US 3) needles for edging
1 pair 4mm (US 6) needles for main body

## Zip
Open-ended zip to fit

## Tension
20 sts and 28 rows to 10cm measured over textured pattern using 4 mm (US 6) needles

## Back
Using 3 ¼ mm (US 3) needles cast on 69,77,85 sts and work from chart and written instructions as folls:
**Chart row 1:** (K1, P1) to last st, K1.
**Chart row 2:** (K1, P1) to last st, K1.
Cont in moss st until chart row 8 completed.
Change to 4mm (US 6) needles and work in in textured star pattern as indicated on chart.
Work until chart row 62,72,80 completed.
**Shape armhole**
Cast off 6 sts at the beg next 2 rows. (57,65,73 sts)

Work until chart row 100,112,122 completed.
**Shape back neck**
**Chart row 101,113,123:** Patt until 18,21,24 sts on RH needle, turn and leave rem sts on a holder.
**Chart row 102,114,124:** Cast off 3 sts, patt to end.
Slip rem 15,18,21 sts onto a holder.
Rejoin yarn and cast off centre 21,23,25, patt to end. (18,21,24 sts)
**Chart row 102,114,124:** Patt 1 row.
**Chart row 103,115,125:** Cast off 3 sts, patt to end.
Slip rem 15,18,21 sts onto a holder.

## Front Pocket Linings (work 2)
Using 4 mm (US 6) needles cast on 19,21,21 sts, beg with a K row work 24,26,28 rows in st st. Leave sts on a holder.

## Left Front
Using 3 ¼ mm (US 3) needles cast on 35,39,43 sts and work from chart and written instructions as folls:
**Note:** 3 sts at centre front are knitted in moss st throughout and are **not** shown on chart.
**Chart row 1:** (K1, P1) to last st, K1.
**Chart row 2:** (K1, P1) to last st, K1.
Cont in moss st until chart row 8 completed.
Change to 4mm (US 6) needles and work from chart for left front as folls:
**Row 11:** Knit to last 2 sts, P1, K1 .
**Row 12:** K1, P1, K1, purl to end.
These 2 rows set the sts.
Cont to work in textured star pattern from chart until row 32,34,36 completed.
**Chart row 33,35,37 (place pocket):** Patt 7,9,11 sts, slip next 19,21,21 sts onto a holder, patt across 19,21,21sts from first pocket linning taking sts into textured star pattern, patt to end.
Cont to work until row 62,72,80 completed.
**Shape armhole**
Cast off 6 sts at the beg next row.
(29,33,37 sts)
Work without further shaping until chart row 93,105,115 completed.
**Shape front neck**
**Chart row 94,106,116:** Patt 8,9,10 sts and slip these onto a holder, patt to end.
(21,24,27 sts)
Work 1 row.
**Chart row 96,108,118:** Cast off 4 sts, patt to end.
Dec 1 st at neck edge on next 2 rows.
(15,18,21 sts)
Work without further shaping until chart row 102,114,124 completed.
Slip rem sts onto a holder.

## Right Front
Using 3 ¼ mm (US 3) needles cast on 35,39,43 sts an work from chart and written instructions as folls:
**Note:** 3 sts at centre front are knitted in moss st throughout and are **not** shown on chart.
**Chart row 1:** (K1, P1) to last st, K1.
**Chart row 2:** (K1, P1) to last st, K1.
Cont in moss st until chart row 8 completed.
Change to 4mm (US 6) needles and work from chart f right front as folls:
**Row 11:** K1, P1, Knit to end.
**Row 12:** Purl to last 3 sts, K1, P1, K1.
These 2 rows set the sts.
Complete to match left front, foll chart for right front ar reversing shaping and placing of pocket.

## Sleeves (both alike)
Using 3 ¼ mm (US 3) needles cast on 35,37,39 sts an work from chart and written instructions as folls:
**Chart row 1:** P1,0,1,(K1,P1) to last 2,1,2 sts. K1, P1,0,1.
**Chart row 2:** P1,0,1,(K1,P1) to last 2,1,2 sts. K1, P1,0,1.
Cont in moss st until chart row 8 completed.
Change to 4 mm (US 6) needles and work in textured star pattern as indicated on chart.
**Chart row 9:** Inc into first st, knit to last st, inc into last st. (37,39,41 sts)
**Chart row 12:** Purl.
Cont in textured star patt from chart, shaping sides by inc as indicated to 55,59,63 sts.
Work without further shaping until chart row 62,70,78 completed. Cast off.

## Press
all pieces as shown in making up instructions, page 48.

## Neckband
Join both shoulder seams using backstitch.
With RS facing and using 3 ¼ mm (US 3) needles worl in patt across 8,9,10 sts on holder at right front neck, pick up and knit 10 sts up right front neck shaping, pick up and knit 27,29,31 sts across back neck, and 10 sts down left front neck, work in patt across 8,9,10 sts on holder. (63,67,71 sts)
Work 6,6,8 rows in moss st ending with a RS row.
Cast off knitwise.

## Making up
**Pocket tops** (both alike)
With RS facing slip 19,21,21 sts left on pocket holder onto 3¼ mm (US 3) needle. Rejoin yarn, work 4 rows in moss st ending with a WS row. Cast off in moss st.
Complete as shown in making up instructions, page 48

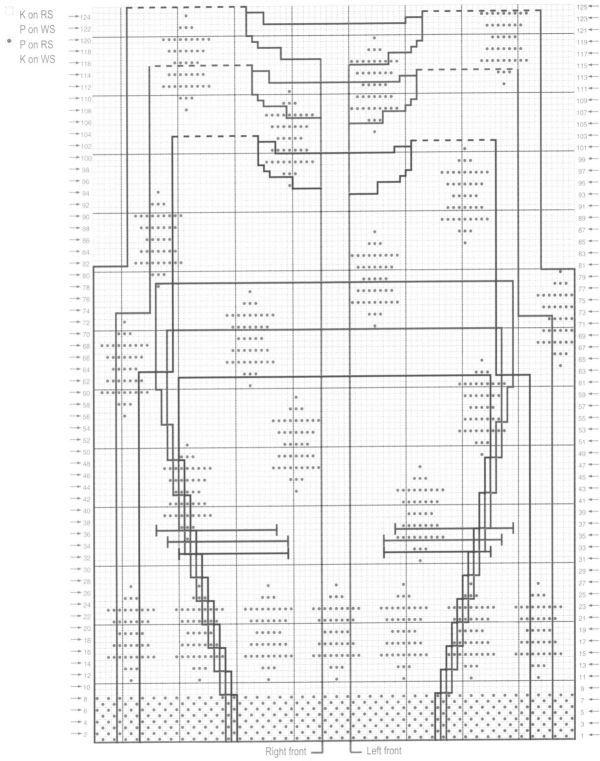

K on RS
P on WS

● P on RS
K on WS

Right front — Left front

33

# Soapy Sweater

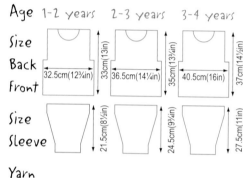

| Age | 1-2 years | 2-3 years | 3-4 years |
|---|---|---|---|
| **Size** | | | |
| **Back** | 32.5cm(12¾in) | 36.5cm(14¼in) | 40.5cm(16in) |
| **Front** | 33cm(13in) | 35cm(13¾in) | 37cm(14½in) |
| **Size** | | | |
| **Sleeve** | 21.5cm(8½in) | 24.5cm(9¾in) | 27.5cm(11in) |

## Yarn

Rowan Handknit Cotton x 50g balls

| Dove | 6 | 6 | 7 |
|---|---|---|---|

## Needles

1 pair 3 ¼ mm (US 3) needles for edging
1 pair 4mm (US 6) needles for main body

## Tension

20 sts and 31 rows to 10cm measured over textured pattern using 4 mm (US 6) needles

## Back

Using 3 ¼ mm (US 3) needles, cast on 65,73,81 sts and work from chart and written instructions as folls:
**Chart row 1:** K1,2,0, P0,1,1, K0,2,2, (K3,P1,K2) 10,11,13 times, K3,2,0, P1,0,0.
**Chart row 2:** P2,0,0, K1,1,0, P1,1,0, (P1,K1,P2,K1,P1) 10,11,13 times, P1,1,1, K0,1,1, P0,2,1, K0,1,0.
Cont in edging patt from chart until row 14 completed. Change to 4mm (US 6) needles and cont to work in patt setting sts as folls:
**Chart row 15:** K5,9,13, (P1,K4) twice, P1,K5,(P1,K1) twice, P1,K13,(P1,K1) twice, P1,K5,(P1,K4) twice, P1, K5,9,13.

**Chart row 16:** P5,9,13, (P1,K1,P2,K1) twice, P5,(K1,P1) twice, P2,K1,P11,K1,P2, (P1,K1) twice, P5,(K1,P2,K1,P1,) twice, P5,9,13.
Work in textured patt from chart until row 66,68,72 completed.

### Shape armhole
Cast off 6 sts at the beg next 2 rows. (53,61,69 sts)
Work until chart row 106,112,118 completed.

### Shape shoulders and back neck
Cast off 4,5,6, sts at the beg next 2 rows.
**Chart row 109,115,121:** Cast off 4,5,6 sts, patt until 6,7,8 sts on RH needle, turn and leave rem sts on a holder.
**Chart row 110,116,122:** Cast off 3 sts, patt to end. Cast off rem 3,4,5 sts.
Slip centre 25,27,29 sts onto a holder, rejoin yarn to rem sts and patt to end.  (10,12,14 sts)
**Chart row 110,116,122:** Cast off 4,5,6 sts, patt to end. (6,7,8 sts)
**Chart row 111,117,123:** Cast off 3 sts, patt to end. Cast off rem 3,4,5 sts.

## Front

Work as for back until chart row 102,108,114 completed.

### Shape front neck
**Chart row 103,109,115:** Patt 17,20,23 sts, turn and leave rem sts on a holder.
**Chart row 104,110,116:** Cast off 4 sts, patt to end. Dec 1 st at neck edge on next 2 rows. (11,14,17 sts)

### Shape Shoulder
**Chart row 107,113,119:** Cast off 4,5,6 sts at beg next row and foll alt row.
Patt 1 row.
Cast off rem 3,4,5 sts.
Slip centre 19,21,23 sts onto a holder, rejoin yarn to rem sts and patt to end.  (17,20,23 sts)
Patt 1 row
**Chart row 105,111,117:** Cast off 4 sts, patt to end. Dec 1 st at neck edge on next 2 rows. (11,14,17 sts)

### Shape shoulder
**Chart row 108,114,120:** Cast off 4,5,6 sts at beg next row and foll alt row.
Patt 1 row.  Cast off rem 3,4,5 sts.

## Sleeves (both alike)

Using 3 ¼ mm (US 3) needles cast on 33,35,37 sts and work from chart and written instructions as folls:
**Chart row 1:** K0,1,2, P1,1,1, K2,2,2, (K3,P1,K2) 5 times, K0,1,2.
**Chart row 2:** K0,0,1, P0,1,1, (P1,K1,P2,K1,P1) 5 times, P1,1,1, K1,1,1, P1,2,2, K0,0,1.

Cont in in edging patt from chart until row 10 complete Change to 4mm (US 6) needles.
**Chart row 11:** Inc into first st, work in patt from chart t last st, inc into last st. (35,37,39 sts)
**Chart row 12:** Patt across row.
Cont in textured patt from chart, shaping sides by inc a indicated to 51,55,59 sts.
Work without further shaping until chart row 70,80,90 completed.
Cast off .

*Press* all pieces as shown in making up instructions, page 48.

## Neckband

Join right shoulder seam using backstitch.
Using 3 ¼ mm (US 3) needles pick up and knit 11 sts down left front neck, knit across 19,21,23 sts on holder pick up and knit 11 sts to shoulder and 3 sts down righ back neck, knit across 25,27,29 sts on holder, pick up and knit 3 sts to shoulder. (72,76,80 sts)
**Rib row 1 (WS row):** K2, P2 to end.
**Rib row 2 (RS row):** K2, P2 to end.
Work these 2 rows 4 times more.
Cast off in rib.
Complete sweater as shown in making up instructions, page 48.

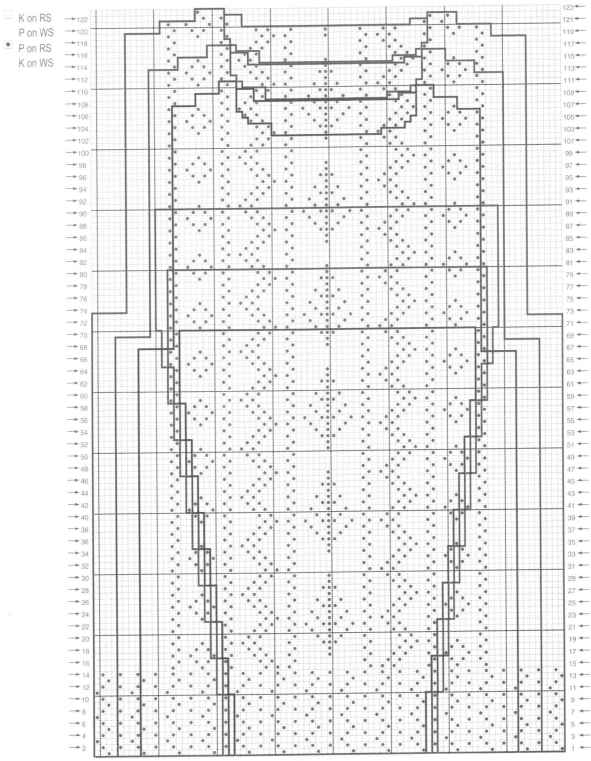

# Big Spot Slipover

## Age
1-2 years    2-3 years    3-4 years

## Size

Back

Front

31cm(12¼in)  30cm(11¾in)    35cm(13¾in)  32cm(12½in)    39cm(15¼in)  34cm(13¼in)

## Yarn
Rowan Handknit Cotton x 50g balls

Deep        3              4              4

## Needles
1 pair 3 ¼ mm (US 3) needles for edging
1 pair 4mm (US 6) needles for main body

## Tension
20 sts and 28 rows to 10cm measured over textured
pattern using 4 mm (US 6) needles

## Back
Using 3 ¼ mm (US 3) needles, cast on 61,69,77 sts and
work from chart and written instructions as folls:
**Chart row 1:** Knit.
**Chart row 2:** Purl.
Work these 2 rows once more.
**Chart row 5:** Knit.
**Chart row 6:** Knit.
Work these 2 rows once more.
Change to 4mm (US 6) needles and cont to work in
textured spot patt as folls:
**Chart row 9:** P0,0,4, K1,5,5, (P11,K5) 3 times, P11,
K1,5,5, P0,0,4.
**Chart row 10:** K0,0,4, P1,5,5, (K11,P5) 3 times, K11,
P1,5,5, K0,0,4.
Work until chart row 56,60,64 completed.

## Shape armhole
Cast off 4 sts at beginning next 2 rows.
(53,61,69 sts)
Dec 1 st at each end of next 3 rows and 2 foll alt rows.
(43,51,59 sts)
### Ages 2-3 years and 3-4 years only
Work 3 rows in st st.
Dec 1 st at armhole edge on next row. (49,57 sts)
### All ages
Work without further shaping to chart row 90,96,102
completed.
## Shape shoulders and back neck
Cast off 4,5,6, sts at the beg next row, patt until 6,7,9
sts on RH needle, turn and leave rem sts on a holder.
**Chart row 92,98,104:** Cast off 3 sts, patt to end.
Cast off rem 3,4,6 sts.
Slip centre 23,25,27 sts onto a holder, rejoin yarn to rem
sts and patt to end.
(10,12,15 sts)
**Chart row 92,98,104:** Cast off 4,5,6 sts, patt to end.
(6,7,9 sts)
**Chart row 93,99,105:** Cast off 3 sts, patt to end.
Cast off rem 3,4,6 sts.

## Front
Work as for back until chart row 84,90,96 completed.
## Shape front neck
**Chart row 85,91,97:** Patt 13,15,18 sts, turn and leave
rem sts on a holder.
**Chart row 86,92,98:** Cast off 4 sts, patt to end.
Dec 1 st at neck edge on next 2 rows.
(7,9,12 sts)
Work 2 rows.
## Shape Shoulder
**Chart row 91,97,103:** Cast off 4,5,6 sts at beg next row.
Patt 1 row.
Cast off rem 3,4,6 sts.
Slip centre 17,19,21 sts onto a holder, rejoin yarn to rem
sts and patt to end.
(13,15,18 sts)
Patt 1 row
**Chart row 87,93,99:** Cast off 4 sts, patt to end.
Dec 1 st at neck edge on next 2 rows. (7,9,12 sts)
Work 2 rows.
## Shape shoulder
**Chart row 92,98,104:** Cast off 4,5,6 sts at beg next row.
Patt 1 row.
Cast off rem 3,4,6 sts.

*Press* all pieces as shown in making up instructions,
page 48.

## Neck Edging
Join right shoulder seam using backstitch.
With RS facing and using 3 ¼ mm (US 3) needles
pick up and knit 10 sts down left front neck, knit
across 17,19,21 sts on holder, pick up and knit 10
sts to shoulder and 3 sts down right back neck, knit
across 23,25,27 sts on holder, pick up and knit 3 sts to
shoulder. (66,70,74 sts)
**Edging row 1 (WS row):** Knit.
Beg with a K row work 5 rows in st st.
Using 4mm (US 6) needle cast off knitwise on WS.
Join left shoulder seam using backstitch.

## Armhole edging (both alike)
With RS facing and using 3 ¼ mm needles and RS of
garment facing pick up and knit 30,32,34 sts from side
seam to shoulder and 30,32,34 sts down to side seam
(60,64,68 sts)
**Edging row 1 (WS row):** Knit.
**Edging row 2 (RS row):** Knit.
Cast off knitwise.
Complete slipover as shown in making up instructions
page 48.

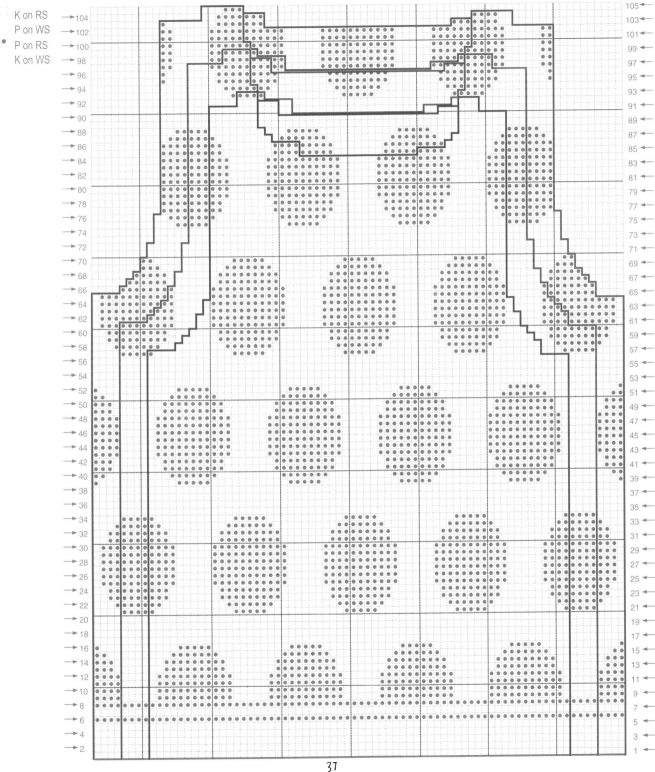

# Silver Splash Jacket

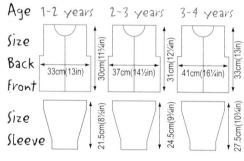

| Age | 1-2 years | 2-3 years | 3-4 years |
|---|---|---|---|
| Size Back Front | 33cm(13in) 30cm(11¾in) | 37cm(14½in) 31cm(12¼in) | 41cm(16¼in) 33cm(13in) |
| Size Sleeve | 21.5cm(8½in) | 24.5cm(9¾in) | 27.5cm(10¾in) |

## Yarn
Rowan Wool Cotton x 50g balls
| Aqua | 5 | 5 | 6 |

## Needles
1 pair 3 ¼ mm (US 3) needles for edging
1 pair 4mm (US 6) needles for main body

## Zip
Open-ended zip to fit

## Tension
21 sts and 32 rows to 10cm measured over textured pattern using 4 mm (US 6) needles

## Back
Using 3 ¼ mm (US 3) needles cast on 69,77,85 sts and work from chart and written instructions as folls:
**Chart row 1:** Knit.
**Chart row 2:** Knit.
**Chart row 3:** K1, P1, to last st, K1.
**Chart row 2:** K1, P1, to last st, K1.
Cont in moss st until chart row 14 completed.
Change to 4mm (US 6) needles work in textured zig zag patt from chart for back.
Work until chart row 58,60,62 completed.

## Shape armhole
Cast off 6 sts at the beg next 2 rows. (57,65,73 sts)
Work until chart row 100,104,110 completed.
## Shape shoulders and back neck
Cast off 5,6,7, sts at the beg next 2 rows.
**Chart row 103,107,113:** Cast off 5,6,7 sts, patt until 7,8,9 sts on RH needle, turn and leave rem sts on a holder.
**Chart row 104,108,114:** Cast off 3 sts, patt to end.
Cast off rem 4,5,6 sts.
Rejoin yarn and cast off centre 23,25,27 sts, patt to end.
**Chart row 104,108,114:** Cast off 5,6,7 sts, patt to end. (7,8,9 sts)
**Chart row 105,109,115:** Cast off 3 sts, patt to end.
Cast off rem 4,5,6 sts.

## Left Front
Using 3 ¼ mm (US 3) needles cast on 34,38,42 sts and work from chart and written instructions as folls:
**Note:** 7 sts at centre front are knitted in moss st throughout and are **not** shown on chart.
**Chart row 1:** Knit.
**Chart row 2:** Knit.
**Chart row 3:** K1, P1 to end.
**Chart row 2:** P1, K1 to end.
Cont in moss st until chart row 14 completed.
Change to 4mm (US 6) needles and work from chart for left front as folls:
**Row 15:** Knit to last 7 sts, (P1, K1) 3 times, P1.
**Row 16:** (P1, K1) 3 times, P1, purl to end.
These 2 rows set the sts.
Work in textured zig zag from chart for left front until chart row 58,60,62 completed.
## Shape armhole
Cast off 6 sts at the beg next row. (28,32,36 sts)
Work until chart row 95,99,105 completed.
## Shape front neck
**Chart row 96,100,106:** Cast off 9,10,11 sts, patt to end. (19,22,25 sts). Work 1 row.
**Chart row 98,102,108:** Cast off 3 sts, patt to end.
Dec 1 st at neck edge on next 2 rows. (14,17,20 sts)
## Shape shoulder
Cast off 5,6,7, sts at the beg next row and foll alt row.
Work 1 row. Cast off rem 4,5,6 sts.

## Right Front
Using 3 ¼ mm (US 3) needles cast on 34,38,42 sts and work from chart and written instructions as folls:
**Note:** 7 sts at centre front are knitted in moss st throughout and are **not** shown on chart.
**Chart row 1:** Knit.
**Chart row 2:** Knit.
**Chart row 3:** P1, K1 to end.

## Chart row 4: K1, P1 to end.
Cont in moss st until chart row 14 completed.
Change to 4mm (US 6) needles and work from chart fc right front as folls:
**Row 15:** (P1, K1) 3 times, P1, knit to end.
**Row 16:** Purl to last 7 sts, (P1, K1) 3 times, P1.
These 2 rows set the sts.
Work textured zig zag patt from chart, complete to match left front, foll chart for right front and reversing shaping.

## Sleeves (both alike)
Using 3 ¼ mm (US 3) needles cast on 35,37,39 sts and work from chart and written instructions as folls:
**Chart row 1:** Knit.
**Chart row 2:** Knit.
**Chart row 3:** K0,1,0 (P1, K1) to last 1,2,1 sts, P1, K0,1,0.
**Chart row 4:** K0,1,0 (P1, K1) to last 1,2,1 sts, P1, K0,1,0.
Work 2 more rows in moss st on sts as set.
**Chart row 7:** Inc into first st, patt to last st, inc into last st. (37,39,41 sts)
**Chart row 8:** Patt to end.
Work 4 more rows in moss st.
**Chart row 13:** Work as row 7. (39,41,43 sts)
Work 1 row.
Change to 4 mm (US 6) needles and cont to work in textured zig zag pattern from chart, shaping sides by in as indicated to 55,59,63 sts.
Work without further shaping until chart row 72,82,92 completed. Cast off.

## Press all pieces as shown on page 48.

## Right Front edging
With RS of right front facing and using 3¼ mm (US 3) needles pick up and knit 67,71,75 sts from cast on edge to start of neck shaping.
Knit 2 rows ending with a RS row. Cast off knitwise.

## Left Front edging
With RS of right front facing and using 3¼ mm (US 3) needles pick up and knit 67,71,75 sts from start of neck shaping to cast on edge.
Knit 2 rows ending with a RS row. Cast off knitwise.

## Collar
Using 3 ¼ mm (US 3) needles cast on 73,77,81 sts.
Work 19,21,23 rows in moss st ending with a RS row.
Knit 2 rows ending with a RS row. Cast off knitwise.
Join both shoulder seams using backstitch.
Sew cast on edge of collar to neck edge, matching row ends at front opening edges.
Complete as shown in making up instructions, page 48

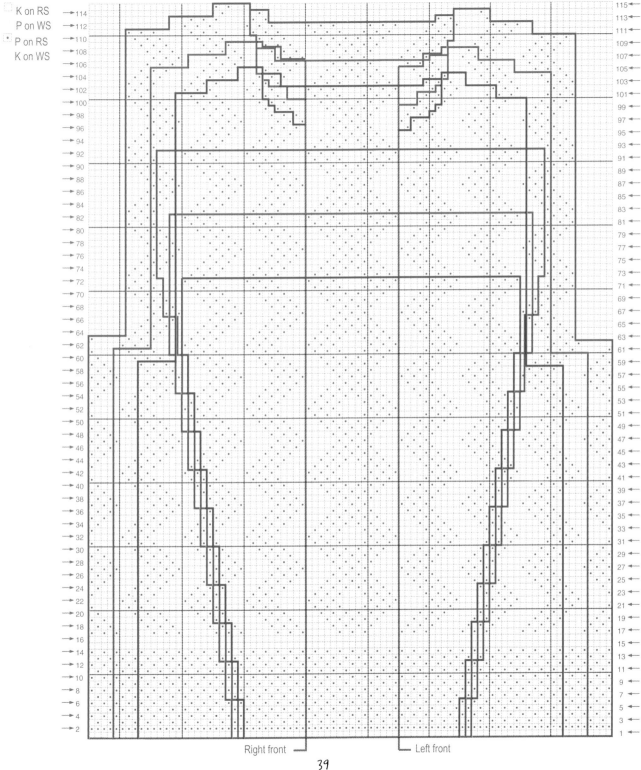

K on RS
P on WS

P on RS
K on WS

Right front      Left front

39

# Hearts Sweater

## Age
1-2 years     2-3 years     3-4 years

## Size
Back
Front

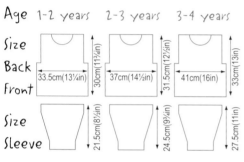

33.5cm(13¼in)    37cm(14½in)    41cm(16in)

30cm(11¾in)    31.5cm(12½in)    33cm(13in)

## Size
Sleeve

21.5cm(8½in)    24.5cm(9¾in)    27.5cm(11in)

## Yarn
Rowan All Seasons Cotton x 50g balls
Cornflower   5       5       6

## Needles
1 pair 4mm (US 6) needles for edging
1 pair 5mm (US 8) needles for main body

## Tension
17 sts and 24 rows to 10cm measured over textured
pattern using 5mm (US 8) needles

## Back
Using 4mm (US 6) needles cast on 57,63,69 sts and
work from chart and written instructions as folls:
**Chart row 1:** K1,0,1, (P1,K1) to last 0,1,0 st, P0,1,0.
**Chart row 2:** K1,0,1, (P1,K1) to last 0,1,0 st, P0,1,0.
Cont in moss st until chart row 8 completed.
Change to 5mm (US 8) needles and work in textured
heart patt as on chart folls:
**Chart row 9:** Purl.
**Chart row 10:** Knit.
Work until chart row 44,46,48 completed.

## Shape armhole
Cast off 5 sts at the beg next 2 rows. (47,53,59 sts)
Work until chart row 74,78,82 completed.
### Shape back neck
**Chart row 75,79,83:** Patt until 13,15,17 sts on RH
needle, turn and leave rem sts on a holder.
**Chart row 76,80,84:** Cast off 3 sts, patt to end.
Slip rem 10,12,14 sts onto a holder.
Slip centre 21,23,25 sts onto a holder, rejoin yarn to
rem sts and patt to end.
(13,15,17 sts)
**Chart row 76,80,84:** Patt 1 row.
**Chart row 77,81,85:** Cast off 3 sts, patt to end.
Slip rem 10,12,14 sts onto a holder.

## Front
Work as for back to chart row 68,72,76 completed.
### Shape front neck
**Chart row 69,73,77:** Patt 16,18,20 sts, turn and leave
rem sts on a holder.
**Chart row 70,74,78:** Cast off 4 sts, patt to end.
Dec 1 st at neck edge on next 2 rows. (10,12,14 sts)
Work without further shaping until chart row
76,80,84 completed.
Slip rem sts onto a holder.
Slip centre 15,17,19 sts onto a holder, rejoin yarn to
rem sts and patt to end.
(16,18,20 sts)
**Chart row 70,74,78:** Patt 1 row.
**Chart row 71,75,79:** Cast off 4 sts, patt to end.
Dec 1 st at neck edge on next 2 rows. (10,12,14 sts)
Work without further shaping until chart row
77,81,85 completed.
Slip rem sts onto a holder.

## Sleeves (both alike)
Using 4mm (US 6) needles cast on 29,31,33 sts and
work from chart and written instructions as folls:
**Chart row 1:** K1,0,1, (P1,K1) to last 0,1,0 sts, P0,1,0.
**Chart row 2:** K1,0,1, (P1,K1) to last 0,1,0 sts, P0,1,0.
Cont in moss st until chart row 8 completed.
Change to 5mm (US 8) needles and work in textured
heart patt as on chart folls:
**Chart row 9:** Inc into first st, purl to last st, inc into
last st. (31,33,35 sts)
**Chart row 10:** knit.
Cont in textured heart patt from chart, shaping sides by
inc as indicated to 45,47,51 sts.
Work without further shaping until chart row
56,62,70 completed. Cast off.

**Press** all pieces as shown in making up instructions,
page 48.

## Neckband
Join right shoulder seam by knitting sts together on the
WS of garment as shown in techniques guide, page 4-
Using 4mm (US 6) needles pick up and knit 10 sts dov
left front neck, knit across 15,17,19 sts on holder, pick
up and knit10 sts to shoulder and 3 sts down right bac
neck, knit across 21,23,25 sts on holder and pick up
and knit 3 sts to shoulder. (62,66,70 sts)
**Edging row 1 (WS):** K1,P1 to end.
**Edging row 2:** P1,K1 to end.
Work these 2 rows once more.
Cast off knitwise.
Join left shoulder seam by knitting sts together on the
WS of garment as above.
Join neckband seam using backstitch.
Complete sweater as shown in making up instructions.
page 48.

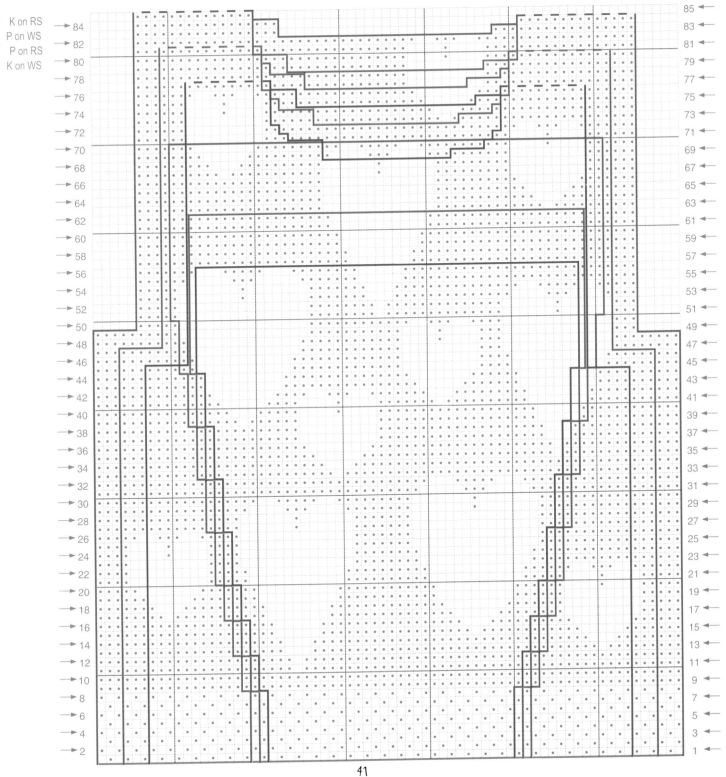

# Digging Sweater

## Age 1-2 years  2-3 years  3-4 years

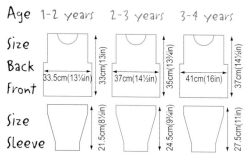

| Size | 33.5cm(13¼in) | 33cm(13in) | 37cm(14½in) | 35cm(13¾in) | 41cm(16in) | 37cm(14½in) |
|------|------|------|------|------|------|------|
| Back |  |  |  |  |  |  |
| Front |  |  |  |  |  |  |

Size Sleeve: 21.5cm(8½in)  24.5cm(9¾in)  27.5cm(11in)

## Yarn

Rowan Wool Cotton x 50g balls
Splash      5        5        6

## Needles

1 pair 3 ¼ mm (US 3) needles for ribs
1 pair 4mm (US 6) needles for main body

## Tension

22 sts and 30 rows to 10cm measured over stocking stitch using 4 mm (US 6) needles

## Back

Using 3 ¼ mm (US 3) needles, cast on 74,82,90 sts and work from chart A and written instructions as folls:
**Note:** 2 sts at each end are knitted in garter st and are **not** shown on the chart.
**Chart row 1:** K6,4,2,(P2, K4) 11,12,14 times, P0,2,2, K2,4,2.
**Chart row 2:** K2, P4,2,0, (K2,P4) 11,12,14 times, K2,2,2, P0,2,0, K0,2,2.
These 2 rows set the sts.
Cont in rib until chart row 16 completed.
Change to 4mm (US 6) needles and cont to work in st st as folls:

**Chart row 17:** Knit.
**Chart row 18:** Purl.
Work until chart row 62,66,70 completed.
Now work from chart B for yoke work 2 rows in st st.
**Shape armhole**
**Chart row 3:** Cast off 6 sts, knit to end.
**Chart row 4:** Cast off 6 sts, knit to end. (62,70,78 sts)
Cont to work in spot pattern until chart row 40,42,44 completed.
**Shape shoulders and back neck**
**Chart row 41,43,45:** Patt until 17,20,23 sts on RH needle, turn and leave rem sts on a holder.
**Chart row 42,44,46:** Cast off 3 sts, patt to end.
Slip rem 14,17,20 sts onto a holder.
Slip centre 28,30,32 sts onto a holder, rejoin yarn to rem sts and patt to end. (17,20,23 sts)
Work 1 row.
**Chart row 43,45,47:** Cast off 3 sts, patt to end.
Slip rem 14,17,20 sts onto a holder.

## Front

Work as for back until row 34,36,38 of chart B completed.
**Shape front neck**
**Chart row 35,37,39:** Patt 20,23,26 sts, turn and leave rem sts on a holder.
**Chart row 36,38,40:** Cast off 4 sts, patt to end.
Dec 1 st at neck edge on next 2 rows. (14,17,20 sts)
Work without further shaping until chart row 42,44,46 completed.
Slip rem sts onto a holder.
Slip centre 22,24,26 sts onto a holder, rejoin yarn to rem sts and patt to end. (20,23,26 sts)
Patt 1 row
**Chart row 37,39,41:** Cast off 4 sts, patt to end.
Dec 1 st at neck edge on next 2 rows. (14,17,20 sts)
Work without further shaping until chart row 43,45,47 completed.
Slip rem sts onto a holder.

## Sleeves (both alike)

Using 3 ¼ mm (US 3) needles cast on 38,40,42 sts and work from chart A and written instructions as folls:
**Chart row 7:** K0,1,2 (P2, K4) 6 times, P2, K0,1,2.
**Chart row 8:** P0,1,2, K2 (P4, K2) 6 times, P0,1,2.
Cont in rib until chart row 16 completed.
Change to 4 mm (US 6) needles and cont to work in st st as folls:
**Chart row 17:** Inc into first st, knit to last st, inc into last st. (40,42,44 sts)
**Chart row 18:** Purl.

Cont in st st from chart, shaping sides by inc as indicated to 58,62,66 sts.
Work without further shaping until chart row 74,84,92 completed.
Cast off .

*Press* all pieces as shown in making up instructions, page 48.

## Neckband

Join right shoulder seam by knitting sts together on the RS of garment as shown in techniques guide, page 48.
With RS facing and using 3 ¼ mm (US 3) needles pick up and knit 8,9,10, sts down left front neck, knit across 22,24,26 sts on holder, pick up and knit 8,9,10 sts to shoulder and 3 sts down right back neck, knit across 28,30,32 sts on holder, pick up and knit 3 sts to shoulder. (72,78,84 sts)
**Rib row 1 (WS row):** K2, P4 to end.
**Rib row 2 (RS row):** K4, P2 to end.
Work these 2 rows 4 times more.
Cast off in rib.
Join left shoulder seam by knitting sts together on the RS of garment as above.
Join neckband seam using backstitch.
Complete sweater as shown in making up instructions, page 48, leaving 16 rows at bottom edge of garment open for side vent.

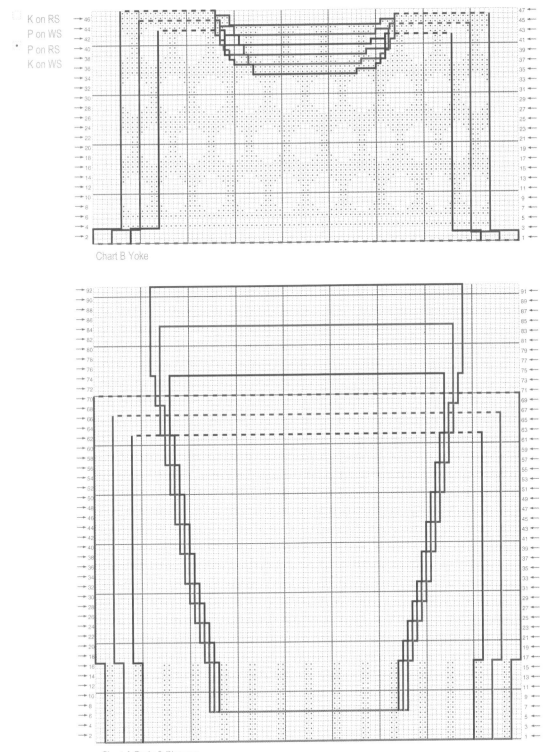

K on RS
P on WS
P on RS
K on WS

Chart B Yoke

Chart A Body & Sleeves

# Windmill Cardigan

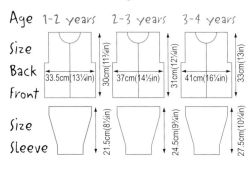

| Age | 1-2 years | 2-3 years | 3-4 years |
|---|---|---|---|
| Size Back Front | 33.5cm(13¼in) 30cm(11¾in) | 37cm(14½in) 31cm(12¼in) | 41cm(16¼in) 33cm(13in) |
| Size Sleeve | 21.5cm(8½in) | 24.5cm(9¾in) | 27.5cm(10¾in) |

## Yarn

Rowan All Seasons Cotton x 50g balls
Iceberg     5             5             6

## Needles

1 pair 4mm (US 6) needles for edging
1 pair 4mm (US 8) needles for main body

## Zip

Open-ended zip to fit

## Tension

17 sts and 24 rows to 10cm measured over stocking stitch using 5mm (US 8) needles

## Back

Using 4mm (US 6) needles cast on 57,63,69 sts and work from chart and written instructions as folls:
**Chart row 1:** P1,0,1, (K1, P1) to last 2,1,2 sts, K1, P1,0,1.
**Chart row 2:** P1,0,1, (K1, P1) to last 2,1,2 sts, K1, P1,0,1.
Cont in moss st until chart row 8 completed.
Change to 5mm (US 8) needles work in textured heart boarder as indicated on chart for back.
Work until chart row 44,46,48 completed.
**Shape armhole**
Cast off 5 sts at the beg next 2 rows. (47,53,59 sts)
Work until chart row 76,80,84 completed.

## Shape shoulders and back neck

Cast off 4,5,5, sts at the beg next 2 rows.
**Chart row 79,83,87:** Cast off 4,5,5 sts, knit until 7,7,9 sts on RH needle, turn and leave rem sts on a holder.
**Chart row 80,84,88:** Cast off 3 sts, purl to end.
Cast off rem 4,4,6 sts.
Rejoin yarn and cast off centre 17,19,21 sts, knit to end.
**Chart row 80,84,88:** Cast off 4,5,5 sts, purl to end. (7,7,9 sts)
**Chart row 81,85,89:** Cast off 3 sts, knit to end.
Cast off rem 4,4,6 sts.

## Left Front

Using 4mm (US 6) needles cast on 25,28,31 sts and work from chart and written instructions as folls:
**Chart row 1:** P1,0,1, (K1, P1) to end.
**Chart row 2:** (P1, K1) to last st, P1,0,1.
These 2 rows set the sts.
Cont until chart row 8 completed.
Change to 5mm (US 8) needles and work in textured heart patt as indicted on chart for left front.
Work until chart row 44,46,48 completed.
**Shape armhole**
Cast off 5 sts at the beg next 2 rows. (20,23,26 sts)
Work until chart row 71,75,79 completed.
**Shape front neck**
**Chart row 72,76,80:** Cast off 3,4,5 sts, patt to end. (17,19,21 sts)
Work 1 row.
**Chart row 74,76,82:** Cast off 3 sts, patt to end.
Dec 1 st at neck edge on next 2 rows. (12,14,16 sts)
**Shape shoulder**
Cast off 4,5,5, sts at the beg next row and foll alt row.
Work 1 row.
Cast off rem 4,4,6 sts.

## Right Front

Using 4mm (US 6) needles cast on 25,28,31 sts and work from chart and written instructions as folls:
**Chart row 1:** (P1, K1) to last st, P1,0,1
**Chart row 2:** P1,0,1, (K1, P1) to end.
These 2 rows set the sts.
Cont until chart row 8 completed.
Change to 5mm (US 8) needles and work in textured heart patt as indicted on chart for right front.
Complete to match left front, foll chart for right front and reversing shaping.

## Sleeves (both alike)

Using 4 mm (US 6) needles cast on 29,31,33 sts and work from chart and written instructions as folls:
**Chart row 1:** P1,0,1, (K1, P1) to last 2,1,2 sts, K1, P1,0,1
**Chart row 2:** P1,0,1, (K1, P1) to last 2,1,2 sts, K1, P1,0,1
Cont in moss st until chart row 8 completed.
Change to 5mm (US 8) needles work in textured heart boarder as indicated on chart for sleeve.
**Chart row 9:** Inc into first st, knit to last st, inc into last st. (31,33,35 sts)
**Chart row 10:** Purl.
Cont in patt from chart, shaping sides by inc as indicated to 45,47,51 sts.
Work without further shaping until chart row 56,62,70 completed.
Cast off.

**Press** all pieces as shown in making up instructions, page 48.

## Buttonhole band

With RS of right front facing and using 4 mm (US 6) needles pick up and knit 49,53,57 sts from cast on edge to start of neck shaping.
**Row 1 (WS row):** (K1, P1) to last st, K1.
**Row 2:** (K1, P1) to last st, K1.
**Buttonhole row (WS row):** Patt 6,7,8, (yo, patt 2tog, patt 11,12,13) 3 times, yo, patt 2tog, patt 2.
Work 2 more rows in moss st.
Cast off in moss st.

## Buttonband

With RS of right front facing and using 4 mm (US 6) needles pick up and knit 49,53,57 sts from start of neck shaping to cast on edge.
**Row 1 (WS row):** (K1, P1) to last st, K1.
Work 4 more rows in moss st.
Cast off in moss st.

## Neckband

Join both shoulder seams using backstitch.
With RS facing and using 4 mm (US 6) needles pick up and knit 5 sts across buttonhole band, 12,13,14 sts up right front neck shaping, 23,25,27 sts across back neck, and 12,13,14 sts down left front neck, and 5 sts from buttonband. (57,61,65 sts)
**Row 1(WS):** (K1, P1) to last st, K1.
Work 1 row in moss st.
**Buttonhole row (WS row):** Patt to last 4 sts, yo, patt 2tog, patt 2.
Work 2 more rows in moss st.
Cast off in moss st.
Complete jacket as shown in making up instructions, page 48.
Sew on buttons to correspond with buttonholes.

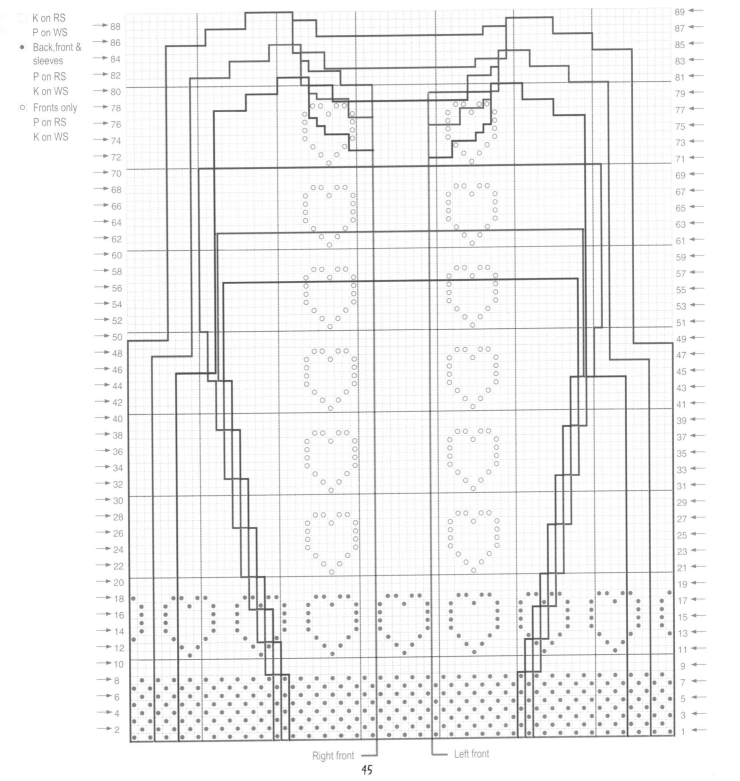

K on RS
P on WS

● Back, front & sleeves
P on RS
K on WS

○ Fronts only
P on RS
K on WS

Right front    Left front

45

# Umbrella Sweater

## Age

| Age | 1-2 years | 2-3 years | 3-4 years |
|-----|-----------|-----------|-----------|

Size Back / Front: 33cm(13in) / 37cm(14½in) / 40cm(15¾in), 33cm(13in) / 35cm(13¾in) / 37cm(14½in)

Size Sleeve: 21.5cm(8½in) / 24.5cm(9¾in) / 28cm(11in)

## Yarn
Rowan All Seasons Cotton x 50g balls

| | | | |
|--|--|--|--|
| Natural | 5 | 5 | 6 |

## Needles
1 pair 4mm (US 6) needles for edging
1 pair 5mm (US 8) needles for main body

## Tension
17 sts and 24 rows to 10cm measured over textured pattern using 5mm (US 8) needles

## Back
Using 4mm (US 6) needles cast on 56,62,68 sts and work from chart and written instructions as foll:
**Chart row 1:** Knit.
**Chart row 2:** Purl.
Work these 2 rows once more.
Change to 5mm (US 8) needles and work textured checker patt setting sts as folls:
**Chart row 5:** P3,6,9, (K10,P10) twice, K10, P3,6,9.
**Chart row 6:** K3,6,9, (P10,K10) twice, P10, K3,6,9.
Work until chart row 52,54,56 completed.

## Shape armhole
Cast off 5 sts at the beg next 2 rows. (46,52,58 sts)
Work until chart row 82,86,90 completed.
## Shape back neck
**Chart row 83,87,91:** Patt until 13,15,17 sts on RH needle, turn and leave rem sts on a holder.
**Chart row 84,88,92:** Cast off 3 sts, patt to end.
Slip rem 10,12,14 sts onto a holder.
Slip centre 20,22,24 sts onto a holder, rejoin yarn to rem sts and patt to end.  (13,15,17 sts)
**Chart row 84,88,92:** Patt 1 row.
**Chart row 85,89,93:** Cast off 3 sts, patt to end.
Slip rem 10,12,14 sts onto a holder.

## Front
Work as for back to chart row 76,80,84 completed.
## Shape front neck
**Chart row 77,81,85:** Patt 16,18,20 sts, turn and leave rem sts on a holder.
**Chart row 78,82,86:** Cast off 4 sts, patt to end.
Dec 1 st at neck edge on next 2 rows. (10,12,14 sts)
Work without further shaping until chart row 84,88,92 completed.
Slip rem sts onto a holder.
Slip centre 14,16,18 sts onto a holder, rejoin yarn to rem sts and patt to end.  (16,18,20 sts)
**Chart row 78,82,86:** Patt 1 row.
**Chart row 79,83,87:** Cast off 4 sts, patt to end.
Dec 1 st at neck edge on next 2 rows. (10,12,14 sts)
Work without further shaping until chart row 85,89,93 completed.
Slip rem sts onto a holder.

## Sleeves (both alike)
Using 4mm (US 6) needles and yarn A cast on 28,30,32 sts and work from chart and written instructions as folls:
**Chart row 1:** Knit.
**Chart row 2:** Purl.
Work these 2 rows once more
Change to 5mm (US 8) needles and work textured checker patt from chart until chart row 8 completed.
**Chart row 9:** Inc into first st, work in patt from chart to last st, inc into last st.
(30,32,34 sts)
**Chart row 10:** Work in patt from chart.
Cont in textured checker patt from chart, shaping sides by inc as indicated to 44,48,52 sts.
Work without further shaping until chart row 56,62,72 completed.
Cast off.

**Press** all pieces as shown in making up instructions, page 48.

## Neckband
Join right shoulder seam by knitting sts together on the RS of garment as shown in techniques guide, page 48.
Using 4mm (US 6) needles pick up and knit 10 sts down left front neck, knit across 14,16,18 sts on holder, pick up and knit 10 sts to shoulder and 3 sts down right back neck, knit across 20,22,24 sts on holder and pick up and knit 3 sts to shoulder. (60,64,68 sts)
Beg with a purl row, work 8 rows in st st ending with a RS row.
Cast off knitwise.
Join left shoulder seam by knitting sts together on the RS of garment as above.
Join neckband seam using backstitch.
Complete sweater as shown in making up instructions, page 48.

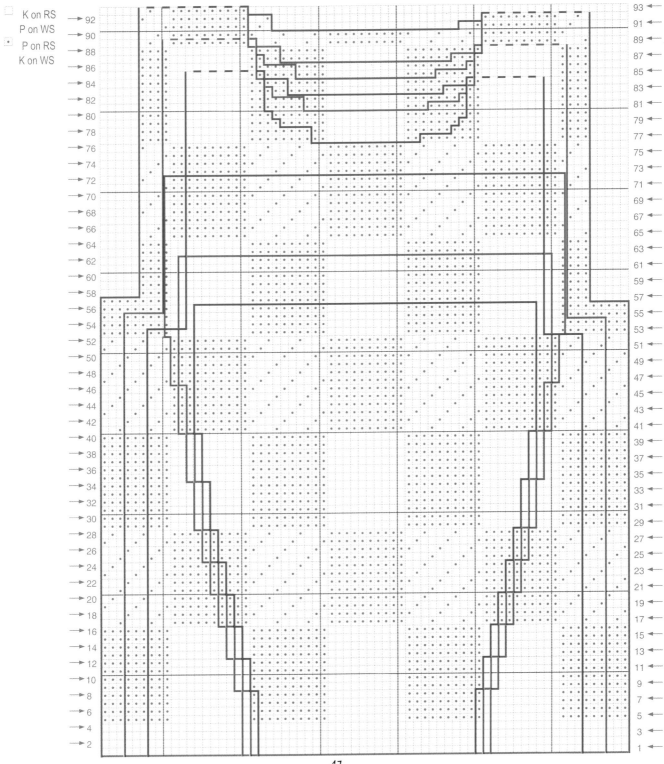

K on RS
P on WS

P on RS
K on WS

47

# Knitting Techniques
## A simple guide to making up and finishing

## Putting your garment together

After spending many hours knitting it is essential that you complete your garment correctly. Following the written instructions and illustrations we show you how easy it is to achieve a beautifully finished garment; which will withstand the most boisterous child.

## Pressing –
With the wrong side of the fabric facing, pin out each knitted garment piece onto an ironing board using the measurements given in the size diagram. As each yarn is different, refer to the ball band and press pieces according to instructions given. Pressing the knitted fabric will help the pieces maintain their shape and give a smooth finish.

## Sewing in ends –
Once you have pressed your finished pieces, sew in all loose ends. Thread a darning needle with yarn, weave needle along approx 5 sts on wrong side of fabric; pull thread through. Weave needle in opposite direction approx 5 sts; pull thread through, cut end of yarn.

## Making Up –
If you are making a sweater join the right shoulder seam as instructed in the pattern, now work the neck edging. Join left shoulder seam and neck edging. If you are making a cardigan, join both shoulder seams as in the pattern and work edgings as instructed. Sew on buttons to correspond with buttonholes. Insert square set in sleeves as follows: Sew cast off edge of sleeve top into armhole. Making a neat right angle, sew in the straight sides at top of sleeve to cast off stitches at armhole. Join side and sleeve seams using either mattress stitch or back stitch. It is important to press each of the seams as you make the garment up.

## Casting Off shoulder Seams together –
This method secures the front and back shoulder stitches together, it also creates a small ridged seam. It is important that the cast off edge should by elastic like the rest of the fabric; if you find that your cast off is too tight, try using a larger needle. You can cast off with the seam on the right side (as illustrated) or wrong side of garment.

1. Place wrong sides of fabric together. Hold both needles with the stitches on in LH, insert RH needle into first stitch on both LH needles.

2. Draw the RH needle through both stitches.

3. Making one stitch on RH needle.

4. Knit the next stitch from both LH needles, two stitches on RH needle.

5. Using the point of one needle in LH, insert into first stitch on RH needle. Take the first stitch over the second stitch.

6. Repeat from 4. until one stitch left on right hand needle. Cut yarn and draw cut end throug stitch to secure.

# cking Up Stitches –

Once you have finished all the garment pieces, pressed them and sewn in all ends, you need to complete the garment by ding a neckband, front bands, or armhole edgings. This is done by picking up stitches along the edge of the knitted piece. The number of stitches to pick up is given in pattern; these are made using a new yarn. When you pick up horizontally along a row of knitting it is important that you pick up through a whole stitch. When picking up ches along a row edge, pick up one stitch in from the edge, this gives a neat professional finish.

Holding work in LH, h RS of fabric facing, ert RH needle into a ole stitch below the st off edge, wrap new n around needle.

2. Draw the RH needle through fabric; making a loop with new yarn on right hand needle.

3. Repeat this action into the next stitch following the pattern instructions until all stitches have been picked up.

4. Work edging as instructed.

# Mattress Stitch –

This method of sewing up is worked on the right side of the fabric and is ideal for matching stripes. Mattress stitch should be worked e stitch in from edge to give the best finish. With RS of work facing, lay the two pieces to be joined edge to edge. Insert needle from WS between edge st and second st. ke yarn to opposite piece, insert needle from front, pass the needle under two rows, bring it back through to the front.

Work mattress stitch undation as above.

2. Return yarn to opposite side working under two rows at a time, repeat..

3. At regular intervals gently pull stitches together.

4. The finished seam is very neat and almost impossible to see.

# ack stitch –

This method of sewing up is ideal for shoulder and armhole seams as it does not allow the fabric to stretch out of shape. Pin the pieces with ht sides together. Insert needle into fabric at end, one stitch or row from edge, take the needle round the two edges securing them. Insert needle into fabric just behind here last stitch came out and make a short stitch . Re-insert needle where previous stitch started, bring up needle to make a longer stitch. Re-insert needle where last itch ended, repeat to end taking care to match any pattern.

# ewing in a Zip –

With right side facing, neatly match row ends and slip stitch fronts of garment together. Pin zip into place, with right side of zip to rong side of garment, matching centre front of garment to centre of zip. Neatly backstitch into place using a matching coloured thread. Undo slip stitches, zip inserted.

# Rowan Overseas Distributors

**AUSTRALIA** : Australian Country Spinners, 314 Albert Street, Brunswick, Victoria 3056. Tel : (03) 9380 3888

**BELGIUM** : Pavan, Koningin Astridlaan 78, B9000 Gent. Tel : (32) 9 221 8594

**CANADA**: Diamond Yarn, 9697 St Laurent, Montreal, Quebec, H3L 2N1. Tel :(514) 388 6188
Diamond Yarn (Toronto), 155 Martin Ross, Unit 3, Toronto, Ontario,M3J 2L9. Tel :(416) 736 6111

**DENMARK** : Please contact Rowan for stockist details.

**FRANCE** : Elle Tricot, 8 Rue du Coq, 67000 Strasbourg. Tel : (33) 3 88 23 03 13.

**GERMANY** : Wolle & Design, Wolfshovener Strasse 76, 52428 Julich-Stetternich. Tel : (49) 2461 54735.
E mail : Wolle_und_Design@t-online.de

**HOLLAND** : de Afstap, Oude Leliestraat 12, 1015 AW Amsterdam. Tel : (31) 20 6231445.

**HONG KONG** : East Unity Co Ltd, Unit B2, 7/F, Block B, Kailey Industrial Centre, 12 Fung Yip Street, Chai Wan. Tel : (852) 2869 7110.

**ICELAND** : Storkurinn, Kjorgardi, Laugavegi 59, Reykjavik. Tel : (354) 551 82 58.

**JAPAN** : Puppy Co Ltd, TOC Building, 7-22-17 Nishigotanda, Shinagawa-ku, Tokyo. Tel : (81) 3 3494 2395.

**KOREA** : My Knit Studio, (3F) 121 Kwan Hoon Dong, Chongro-ku, Seoul. Tel : (82) 2 722 0006

**NEW ZEALAND** : Please contact Rowan for stockist details.

**NORWAY** : Pa Pinne, Tennisvn 3D, 0777 Oslo. Tel : (47) 909 62 818.
E mail : design@paapinne.no

**SWEDEN** : Wincent, Norrtulsgaten 65, 11345 Stockholm. Tel : (46) 8 673 70 60.

**TAIWAN** : Il Lisa International Trading Co Ltd, No 181, Sec 4, Chung Ching N. Road, Taipei, Taiwan R.O.C. Tel : (886) 2 8221 2925.
Chien He Wool Knitting Co, 10 -1 313 Lane, Sec 3, Cmung-Ching North Road, Taipei, Taiwan. Tel : (886) 2 2598 6581

**U.S.A.**: Rowan USA, 4 Townsend West, Suite 8, Nashua, New Hampshire 03063. Tel : (1 603) 886 5041 / 5043.
E mail : wfibers@aol.com

**UNITED KINGDOM** : Green Lane Mill, Holmfirth,West Yorkshire, HD9 2DX. Tel : (44) (0) 1484 681881.
Email : mail@knitrowan.com